Exploring Infrastructure

TUNNELS

Kevin Reilly

Enslow Publishing
101 W. 23rd Street
Suite 240
New York, NY 10011
USA
enslow.com

Published in 2020 by Enslow Publishing, LLC.
101 W. 23rd Street, Suite 240, New York, NY 10011

Copyright © 2020 by Enslow Publishing, LLC.

Library of Congress Cataloging-in-Publication Data

Names: Reilly, Kevin, author.
Title: Tunnels / Kevin Reilly.
Description: New York : Enslow Publishing, 2020. | Series: Exploring infrastructure | Audience: Grades 3 to 6. | Includes bibliographical references and index.
Identifiers: LCCN 2018020367| ISBN 9781978503380 (library bound) | ISBN 9781978505131 (pbk.)
Subjects: LCSH: Tunnels—Juvenile literature. | CYAC: Tunnels. | LCGFT: Instructional and educational works.
Classification: LCC TA807 .R44 2019 | DDC 624.1/93—dc23
LC record available at https://lccn.loc.gov/2018020367

Printed in the United States of America

To Our Readers: We have done our best to make sure all website addresses in this book were active and appropriate when we went to press. However, the author and the publisher have no control over and assume no liability for the material available on those websites or on any websites they may link to. Any comments or suggestions can be sent by email to customerservice@enslow.com.

Photo Credits: Cover, p. 1 gyn9037/Shutterstock.com; cover, pp. 1, 3 (top) Panimoni/Shutterstock.com; p. 5 apiguide/Shutterstock.com; p. 6 Sasa Dzambic Photography/Shutterstock.com; p. 9 Botond Horvath/Shutterstock.com; p. 11 Spumador/Shutterstock.com; p. 12 Rod Morata/Moment Mobile/Getty Images; p. 14 Monty Rakusen/Cultura/Getty Images; p. 17 David McNew/Getty Images; pp. 19, 36 The Asahi Shimbun/Getty Images; p. 23 dpa picture alliance/Alamy Stock Photo; p. 25 Stephen Brashear/Getty Images; p. 28 Bloomberg/Getty Images; p. 33 qaphotos.com/Alamy Stock Photo; p. 34 Angel Franco/The New York Times; p. 40 Tim Boyle/Getty Images; p. 42 Paul Fearn/Alamy Stock Photo; p. 43 Lee Yiu Tung/Shutterstock.com.

CONTENTS

INTRODUCTION: 4

Chapter 1: THE FIRST TUNNELS 8

Chapter 2: TECHNOLOGY CHANGES THE WAY
WE BUILD TUNNELS 15

Chapter 3: WHO BUILDS TUNNELS? 22

Chapter 4: THE WORLD'S COOLEST TUNNELS 31

Chapter 5: WHEN DISASTER STRIKES TUNNELS . . 38

CHRONOLOGY 45

GLOSSARY 46

FURTHER READING 47

INDEX 48

INTRODUCTION

Building Ancient Tunnels:
A Difficult and Important Job

T unnels are wonderful problem solvers. These important structures have many different uses. But they almost always help people solve a problem. A tunnel is any man-made underground passage longer than 75 feet (23 meters) and more than 5.9 feet (1.8 m) wide. For thousands of years, humans have built these structures to make their lives easier. Tunnels can help people reach underground minerals. They allow them to travel through difficult terrain. Tunnels also help people move drinking water and waste materials where they need to go. In this book, we will learn all about tunnels and the people who design and create them.

Today, building simple tunnels is easy. We have huge machines that bore perfect holes into the sides of mountains. We also have advanced explosives and strong materials that help keep tunnels from collapsing and causing accidents. But people have been

Tunnels allow people to travel through areas that would be difficult to cross otherwise.

building tunnels for thousands of years. Those early people did not have any of those things to help them make tunnels.

Try to imagine what it was like to be a tunnel builder three thousand years ago. You do not have dump trucks and cranes. You don't even have electricity! If you're lucky, maybe you have a basic shovel or pick to help move rocks and soil. If not, you have to dig at the sides of the tunnel with your bare hands until you remove enough rocks to carry away from the construction site. As the tunnel gets deeper, the sunlight no longer makes it inside, so you have to work

Building a tunnel is challenging and sometimes dangerous work.

by the light of torches or in complete darkness. It takes months for many tunnel builders to construct even a very short tunnel.

The work is hard, it takes a lot of time, and it's dangerous. People don't know enough about building tunnels to know how to make strong walls and ceilings. Because of this, cave-ins are common. Some people are injured or even killed by these collapses. Others might get trapped inside of the tunnel on the other side of the rubble. Rescuing stranded miners is very difficult, even with today's technology. In the past, it was almost impossible. You know that every time you go to work, you're one false step away from being hurt, trapped, or killed if something goes wrong.

You may be wondering why you should keep building tunnels if it is such a dangerous and difficult job. The answer is that the tunnels are very important for the lives of your families and friends in nearby towns. The earliest tunnels were used for irrigation. Irrigation is a way of watering crops with manmade structures. Tunnels also helped to bring drinking water to townspeople. They were mostly built in the deserts of the Middle East, where the only available water was deep underground. Your job may be dangerous, but it is also very, very important. Without a new tunnel, your town might run out of drinking water before long. So you dig and dig for months, until you finally hit water and save the whole community. Once you're finished, you'll have some time to rest and enjoy the fruits of your labor before it's time to start all over again and dig the next tunnel.

We have improved every aspect of tunnel building since then. But to really appreciate these wonderful structures, it's important to take a look at how they were built thousands of years ago. Let's learn more about ancient tunnels.

Chapter 1

THE FIRST TUNNELS

As you learned in the introduction, tunnels are underground passages with openings on either side. Humans first started to build tunnels thousands of years ago. The tunnels helped them move people and resources through difficult terrain. Today, tunnels have become much more advanced. But we still use them for many of the same reasons.

Ancient Tunnels

Some of the first tunnels were part of aquaducts. These structures were useful for people who lived in dry places. Aqueducts were used to help irrigate crops and transport drinking water. Often, aqueducts would start high up in the mountains. They depended on gravity to bring water from snowcaps and underground streams called aquifers. The water would go all the way down into the town below. Ancient Romans invented concrete, which they used to build aqueducts. These aqueducts lasted for a very long time. Their ruins can be found throughout Europe today. A few of them are even still working!

Another thing that ancient tunnels were used for was basic sewer systems. The earliest known sewer system in the world was built in Persepolis, Iran, in 518 BCE. Workers dug out a complicated network of tunnels into the wall of a mountain bordering the town.

This Roman aqueduct bridge in Spain is several thousand years old. It carried water from a river to a nearby city.

Qanats

As you have learned, people who lived near mountains built aqueducts to transport water. But what did people in the desert do? They invented qanats. These were gently sloping underground tunnels. They used a series of wells to move water up to the surface for drinking and irrigation. Building these structures was complicated work. The skilled workers in charge of designing and constructing them were called muqannīs. It was a high-paying job that was passed down through families from generation to generation. The deepest qanat was in the city of Gonabad in Iran. It still serves forty thousand people after 2,700 years! It is 1,180 feet (360 m) deep and 28 miles (45 kilometers) long.

They filled them in with rubble and soil. This would filter and eliminate the waste. What's most amazing is that the workers did all of this using only hand tools!

Finally, ancient tunnels were used to improve transportation. Suppose someone wanted to travel to a town on the opposite side of some mountains. Before tunnels, that person could either climb the mountain or walk around until they found a good mountain pass. Tunnels allowed ancient travelers to move straight through a mountain. This helped them get where they were going much faster.

The ancient Romans ruled over a huge area that stretched from England to Africa. They wanted to create a network of roads that would connect their empire. One of the first major

An ancient qanat in Iran. These tunnels moved water up to the surface from below ground.

roads they completed was called the Via Flaminia. It used a tunnel to pass through the mountains at one location. The Romans were well known for their construction skills, and their roads and tunnels stood the test of time. Even though that tunnel was finished in 76 CE, you can still drive through it today!

How Do We Use Tunnels Today?

Thousands of years have passed since tunnels were first invented. But we still use them for mostly the same reasons today. Tunnels are usually built for transportation, moving resources, or getting resources. Depending on what they are being used for, some tunnels are built a little differently from others.

The Holland Tunnel carries almost one hundred thousand vehicles into and out of Manhattan every day.

The first major use of tunnels is for transportation. Tunnels that are built for this purpose usually have roads, train tracks, or canals running through them. This is the most common type of this structure that people use on a daily basis. Have you ever driven through some mountains or under a river? If you have, then you've seen the benefits of these tunnels. They let us drive to hard-to-reach places with ease. Without tunnels, no one would be able to cross the Rocky Mountains to reach California without an airplane ticket or a lot of climbing gear!

Just like in ancient times, the second common purpose for modern tunnels is getting resources. Some of the most important needs for human life, like water and fuel, are also the most difficult things for people to access. Miners can use tunnels to travel really deep under the ground. There they can find the coal and other fossil fuels that we use to power our cars and heat our houses. In places that don't have easy access to water, we still use tunnels to get drinking water from underground aquifers. Tunnels that are built to access resources may not be as large as those used for transportation. They might only have a small path for workers to walk on, instead of a multilane highway.

The final major use of tunnels is moving resources. After all, getting them is only half the battle. They also have to be moved to the people who need to use them! Tunnels have solved this problem for many different industries. The best example is the aquifers you

A worker in a mine cutting coal. Miners depend on tunnels to get to resources that are deep underground.

learned about earlier in this chapter. Although aquifers were much more popular thousands of years ago, plenty of working examples of these structures exist today!

Now you know a little more about the early history and basic uses of tunnels. Let's take a closer look at how modern technology has improved them over time.

Chapter 2

TECHNOLOGY CHANGES THE WAY WE BUILD TUNNELS

We build tunnels today for many of the same reasons our ancestors built them. What *has* changed a great deal is how we build our tunnels. Improvements in technology mean that it is much easier to build tunnels today. This chapter will focus on the different ways of constructing modern tunnels. We'll also look at the cutting-edge technologies that engineers use to complete these projects more quickly and safely than ever before!

How Do We Build Tunnels Today?

Tunnels are created using three main methods: cut-and-cover, boring, and immersed tube. Each of these methods has advantages and disadvantages. Now that we have perfected all three, engineers can choose the way that works best for each of their tunnel projects.

The most basic way to build a tunnel is using the cut-and-cover method. This is the way that most tunnels were created in ancient times. First, a long ditch called a trench is dug in the area where the tunnel will be located. Once the trench is finished, workers cover it with a sturdy roof. This roof must be able to support the weight of whatever might go on top of it. The trench needs to be dug very deeply. This ensures that a proper roof can be built while still leaving space for a tunnel underneath. This type of tunnel was so common in the past because it was simple. It also didn't require heavy machinery to build. However, it usually costs a lot of money. It also disrupts traffic in the tunneling area for long periods of time. For these reasons, the cut-and-cover method is not used as much today.

The second modern method of building tunnels is called the boring method. But don't let the name fool you—it's a lot more interesting than it sounds! Instead of digging an open trench, workers dig a tunnel straight through the ground or the side of a mountain. They do this using gigantic boring machines. This method is great because it doesn't cause too much traffic or disrupt the people who

A boring machine breaks through after drilling a 4-mile (6.4-km) tunnel under a mountain range in California.

must get around the area. The boring method is also quicker and costs less than the cut-and-cover method. Only a few skilled workers are needed to operate heavy machinery, instead of an army of people with shovels. However, the boring machines themselves are massive and expensive. This makes them challenging to get and move around.

Tunnel-Boring Machines

Tunnel-boring machines are sometimes called "moles" by workers. They have large, circular faces, called cutter heads, that rotate. The rest of the machine is a powerful thrust system that allows the cutter head to bore through any material, from sand to hard stone. All tunnel boring machines are huge, but the largest one in the world is called the Martina. This monster of an invention weighs 4,500 tons (4,082 metric tons). It can bore a tunnel that is 51 feet (15.5 m) wide!

The last common way to build modern tunnels is the immersed tube method. It is a very popular way to build underwater tunnels. This method has only become possible recently, thanks to advances in technology. A huge tube is built in pieces away from the construction site. Then it is brought to its final location and sunk to the bottom of the water. Once it has been put in the correct position, workers link the sections of tubing together. Finally, they pump the water out of the new tunnel. This method is one of the fastest and cheapest ways to build tunnels, but it only works for underwater structures.

How Has Technology Improved Tunnel Construction?

We've come a long way from building tunnels with shovels and buckets. Over the years, many tools and techniques have been developed to make tunnel construction easier, safer, and faster.

This tunneling shield is the largest in Japan. It is being used to build a 9-mile (16-km) tunnel to connect two highways.

You just learned a bit about tunnel-boring machines. These amazing machines were not made out of thin air. First, a British inventor named Sir Marc Isambard Brunel created tunneling shields. These large cylindrical structures supported tunnel walls as they were being built. Workers would put the shields into place and dig around them. As they made progress, they would push them forward. The shape of the shield would keep the tunnel walls in place until permanent supports could be built. This helped to prevent cave-ins and saved countless lives. Tunnel-boring machines are basically tunneling shields with sharp faces and powerful motors behind them. They also would not exist without Brunel's invention.

Another part of tunnel building that has improved since ancient times is the materials that are used. Today's materials are much stronger and efficient. This means they are better able to support the tunnel's shape. Ancient Romans invented concrete, which they mixed and layered by hand. In 1907, an American named Carl Akeley invented shotcrete. This is concrete that is sprayed from a hose onto a surface at a high speed. Modern construction workers can use shotcrete to quickly solidify the walls of tunnels as they dig. This makes the walls many times stronger and almost eliminates the possibility of cave-ins.

The final improvement that we'll learn about is still years away from being used successfully. It is a new type of tunnel called the submerged floating tunnel. Today, all underwater tunnels are fastened to the bottom of a river, lake, or ocean. This design works well for many situations. But it does not work well in very, very deep water. In those situations, engineers are forced to build bridges. Bridges are much more expensive than tunnels, especially if they need to cover a large distance. A submerged floating tunnel would solve this problem. It would be anchored below the surface of the water deeply enough to avoid boat traffic, but not too deep to cause problems for construction. Proposals for this type of tunnel have been made since the 1800s, but none have ever been built. A company chaired by billionaire Richard Branson has submitted a proposal for this kind of structure. Keep your eyes peeled! You might see the first-ever submerged floating tunnel become reality.

Chapter 3

WHO BUILDS TUNNELS?

Now you know about all of the different ways to construct tunnels. You've learned about the technology that has improved tunnel building and design. It's time to take a look at the most important part of any infrastructure project: the workers!

In ancient times, serious construction projects like tunnels called for hundreds of laborers. They would work for months or years in dangerous conditions. Most of these workers were not highly skilled. They only needed to know how to dig with a shovel and carry a bucket.

In some places, like the deserts of Persia, building tunnels was more complicated. These projects needed skilled workers like the muqannīs who were experts at building qanats. But even though they were trained in digging the tunnels and wells, there were many things they did not know. Most muqannīs had not studied geology,

A worker sprays shotcrete to strengthen the walls of a tunnel.

physics, mathematics, and many other fields that are very important to tunnel construction. This probably led to qanats being built in the wrong places and cave-ins that could have been avoided. Maybe their tunnels would have been more efficient if they were slightly steeper or more level.

Today, we have changed the way that we train workers. We make sure that every possibility is planned for before starting a construction project. Let's learn more about some of the most interesting and important careers that are involved in creating modern tunnels.

Project Planning, Tunnel Design, and Preparations

The most important workers behind any infrastructure project are civil engineers. These are the engineers who design and maintain roads, bridges, tunnels, and other public works. They need to make tons of decisions long before the first piece of dirt is moved for a new tunnel.

Let's say that a city on a river wants to add a new structure to help people get across the water easier. First, civil engineers must decide if a tunnel is even the best structure for the job. In some cases, they may find that a bridge would work better. They also look at how long the project will take. They figure out how many workers and how much material will be needed. They decide which

Surveyors in Seattle, Washington, evaluate a location where a new tunnel will be built.

Environmental Engineers

The environmental engineer is another type of engineer that is very important to any infrastructure project. These highly trained workers figure out what kind of effect the project will have on the environment. They look at the construction as well as the maintenance of the structure. They study the proposed construction site, design plans, and methods the civil engineers are planning to use. In some cases, projects will cause a lot of pollution to the land, air, or water. Environmental engineers can suggest different, safer ways that the construction team could proceed. They might even cancel the project completely until it is brought up to proper environmental standards.

machines will have to be used and how much land will be taken over by the construction site. Each of these factors costs money. The engineers must decide if building a tunnel would be cheaper and more efficient than building a bridge. If so, then that is the structure they'll recommend to the government. At that point, there are almost always some political arguments about costs and benefits. Finally, the funding is approved. That means that we are ready to move on to the next phase of the project: design.

Architects, civil engineers, surveyors, and geologists will all examine the construction site using their own specialties. They will figure out which method of tunnel construction is best. This decision is based on many factors. They have to look at the ground conditions as well as the groundwater conditions. They think about how big the final tunnel is going to be. They consider the difficulties of excavating the tunnel based on the surroundings. Then, they all report their findings to the head engineer in charge of the project. He or she makes the final decision.

At last, everyone is on the same page and all of the paperwork has been approved. The proper machinery is gathered, and a team of workers is created. Now they're ready to actually build the tunnel!

Tunnel Construction and Maintenance

During the construction of the tunnel, several civil engineers are on-site at all times. It is their job to oversee all of the teams involved in the project. They make sure that the workers are following the tunnel plans exactly as they are written. From time to time, they inspect the tunnel as it is being built. They need to make sure that there aren't any problems with the structure that could lead to a cave-in or another type of accident.

At this stage, teams of general construction workers are also a major part of the project. They may not have the same knowledge as the civil engineers. But these construction workers are very different from the laborers of ancient times. The differences are due to technology. First, there are far fewer workers needed to build tunnels than there were in the past. Today's

Many workers and a lot of equipment are needed
to build a tunnel like this one in Malaysia.

heavy machinery can do the work of fifty people with only one or two operators. Second, today's construction workers need to know how to operate the heavy machinery in order to do their jobs well. All of the usual machines from any construction site—like dump trucks, backhoes, and cranes—are used when building tunnels. Construction workers are responsible for using them correctly.

There is another important group besides the general construction workers and the civil engineers. These are the construction workers who specialize in operating the heavy machinery that is used to build tunnels. There are a few kinds of these machines. Which do you think is the most important one? That's right: tunnel-boring machines! There are construction workers who are specially trained to operate them. These workers travel from tunnel site to tunnel site. This is a much better way than teaching general workers how to operate them whenever they are needed. It is smarter and safer to have experts who have many years of practice with these machines.

Finally, the tunnel is finished. Nobody was hurt, and the project was completed ahead of schedule! But the engineer's job is not done yet, even though the tunnel is. Structural engineers will still visit the tunnel from time to time. They need to inspect it and make sure that no repairs need to be done. If they spot an issue, the tunnel may be closed down and a new construction crew will come in to make the necessary repairs.

As you can see, it takes a lot of hard work from many talented people to build a single tunnel. The next time that you're driving through one, take a close look. Think of all the time and energy that went into building it, all so that you could reach your destination a little more quickly!

Chapter 4

THE WORLD'S COOLEST TUNNELS

Now that you are a tunnel expert, let's take a look at some of the most unique and impressive tunnels that the world has to offer. These are the longest, deepest, most mind-boggling tunnels ever built. They hold world records and compete with each other for bragging rights. Who knows, maybe you live close to a record-breaking tunnel and you don't even know it!

The Channel Tunnel

The Channel Tunnel is definitely one of the coolest tunnels on the planet. Its nickname is the Chunnel. It is a submerged tube tunnel

tunnel that crosses the English Channel underwater. It connects England with France. Not long ago, if you told somebody that you were going to go by car from England to France, they would have called you crazy. But today, it is a reality. The tunnel carries twenty-one million passengers and 20 million tons (18.1 million metric tons) of freight between the two countries every year. The Chunnel is 31.4 miles (50 km) long. Its underwater section stretches for 23.5 miles (37.8 km). This makes it the world's longest undersea section of a tunnel.

The Delaware Aqueduct

You don't need to travel to Europe to see a record-breaking tunnel. New York's Delaware Aqueduct is the world's longest tunnel. It is an amazing 85 miles (137 km) long. The aqueduct was built between 1939 and 1945. It carries 1.3 billion gallons (4.9 billion liters) of drinking water from the Catskills Mountains to New York City every day. That means that this tunnel provides more than half of the city's total water supply. But it isn't all good news. The aqueduct has been leaking 36 million gallons (136 million liters) of water per day. A billion-dollar project to repair the leaks has been started. Remember the engineers you learned about in the previous chapter? These are the people who identified the problem and helped figure out how to solve it.

A high-speed train arrives in France after traveling through the Channel Tunnel from the United Kingdom.

The Gotthard Base Tunnel

Another amazing record-breaking tunnel has only existed for a couple of years. The Gotthard Base Tunnel is a railway tunnel that travels beneath the Alps in Switzerland. When it opened at the end of 2016, it became the longest and the deepest transit tunnel on Earth! It is 35.5 miles (57 km) long, and it is the very first flat route through any mountain range. A total of 28 million tons (25.4 million metric tons) of rock were dug up from the mountains during construction. This is as much as the five

A section of the new Delaware Aqueduct bypass is being built
to avoid the area of the original aqueduct that is leaking.

Pyramids of Giza! It took seventeen years to build and cost $9.5 billion. Nine workers died during the building process.

The Seikan Tunnel

The Seikan Tunnel in Japan is not the longest or deepest tunnel in the world. But it is a close second in so many categories that it deserves a spot among the greatest. The tunnel opened in 1988. It connects the islands of Honshu and Hokkaido by underwater railway. The tunnel is 33.4 miles (54 km) long, 330 feet (100 m) below the seabed, and 790 feet (240 m) below sea level. It is the world's longest tunnel with an undersea segment (the Chunnel is shorter, but its undersea segment is longer). The Seikan Tunnel used to be the longest and deepest tunnel in

The Plan to Fix the Aqueduct

New York has decided to build a 2.5-mile-long (4 km) bypass tunnel that will move water around the leaky part of the Delaware Aqueduct. This will allow engineers to fix the source of the leak. Construction on this bypass tunnel began in 2013. It isn't expected to be finished until at least 2021. This is a very complicated project. The entire aqueduct will have to be shut down for a short period of time to make the final connections to the bypass. This will cut off half of New York City's water supply for a short time. Engineers are trying to come up with different ways to make up for this issue.

Tourists take of the Seikan Tunnel in Japan. It is the world's longest tunnel with an underwater segment.

the world. The Gotthard Base Tunnel broke both records when it opened in 2016.

Future Record-Breaker: The Yunnan-Guizhou Water Tunnel

The Yunnan-Guizhou Water Tunnel is surrounded by mystery. The Chinese government denies that the project exists. But experts say that construction on this huge tunnel began in 2017. They say that it is designed to push the Tibet River into the Xinjiang Desert. The goal is to turn the desert into a tropical paradise. An irrigation project of this scale has never been tried before. The tunnel is supposed to be completed around the year 2025. When it's finished, it will supposedly be 410.7 miles (661 km) long. That's nearly five times longer than the current record-holder, the Delaware Aqueduct! Keep an eye out for developments on this story. If it goes according to plan, it is going to be one incredible tunnel.

Chapter 5

WHEN DISASTER STRIKES TUNNELS

You've learned a lot about the good that tunnels can do for communities. You've seen the ways that safety standards have improved over time. But it is important to keep in mind that any major piece of infrastructure should be treated with respect and caution. Accidents do not happen often, but when they do, they tend to be tragedies. This final chapter will profile a few of the worst disasters involving tunnels in recent history. We should always remember that these huge structures should not be treated as if they are indestructible.

The Chicago Flood of 1992

One of the worst accidents involving an American tunnel happened in Chicago, Illinois, in April of 1992. Workers were repairing the Kinzie Street Bridge over the Chicago River. They decided that it needed new pilings. The pilings are the long columns that support the bridge. City officials told the construction company to replace the old pilings with new ones. The construction company was worried that this would damage a nearby building. They asked if they could place the new pilings 3 feet (1 m) over instead. They received permission. Unfortunately, nobody realized that an old abandoned tunnel was located under the water there.

Thankfully, the new pilings that construction workers drove into the ground did not puncture the old tunnel. But installing the pilings shifted a large amount of clay, which eventually got into the tunnel. Muddy water slowly began to leak into it. A worker following a cable into the tunnel came upon the leak. He sent a video of the situation to the city. The city did not think it looked like an emergency, so it took its time finding a company to fix it.

In the meantime, the rest of the mud had pushed through into the tunnel. The Chicago River came rushing into the tunnel at full force. Within minutes, the bottom floors of the whole neighborhood were flooded with 250 million gallons (946.3 million liters) of water. Some buildings had up to 40 feet (12 m) of water in their

This area of the Chicago River under the Kinzie Street Bridge is where the Chicago Flood of 1992 started. Workers unknowingly created a leak in an old underwater tunnel, which ended up causing the huge flood.

lower levels. The entire district was evacuated. Power and gas were cut off to the area as a safeguard. By the time the source of the leak was finally found, the hole in the side of the tunnel was 20 feet (6 m) wide. Workers tried to plug it up with sixty-five dump trucks worth of rocks, cement, and old mattresses. Eventually, a special mixture of concrete was poured directly on the hole, which finally stopped the leak.

It took three days to repair enough flood damage for the area businesses to reopen. This cost the city almost $2 billion. Thankfully, no one was killed in the incident. But if the same thing had happened to a transportation tunnel, the story could have been far more tragic.

The Balvano Train Disaster

There are few tragedies that involve the failure of tunnels. This is thanks to all of the workers who build and maintain them. However, even if tunnels are built perfectly, disasters can still happen.

The Balvano train disaster was the worst rail accident in Italian history. It was also one of the all-time worst rail accidents in the world. In the spring of 1944, World War II was drawing to a close. The Allies had already defeated the government that controlled Italy at the time. There were major shortages of goods. Many people were illegally stowing away on freight trains to travel out to the country. There, they would load up on produce and come back on

Hundreds of people departed on a train from the Balvano train station, shown here, on March 2, 1944. The overloaded train met with one of the worst railway disasters in history.

another train to trade the food with soldiers for supplies. Good coal was also in very short supply. This meant that trains were burning very dirty coal. The coal produced a lot of carbon monoxide, which is a very dangerous gas.

On the night of March 2, 1944, a train passed through the Armi tunnel. It was overloaded with illegal passengers. Because of the extreme weight, the train stalled on a steep hill while almost every car was inside the tunnel. There were drivers at each end of the train. Each one tried to pull the train in a different direction. One pushed forward, while the other tried to back the train out of the tunnel. They weren't able to communicate with each other. Before long, the train workers and most of the passengers had died from carbon monoxide poisoning from the dirty coal smog that filled the tunnel. In the end, 517 people died and 90 survived with severe poisoning.

Advances in technology have made tunnels and rail travel much safer than ever before.

Nobody wanted to claim responsibility for the disaster. Several lawsuits went back and forth without any outcome. But a strict weight limit was placed on the train line from then on, as well as several other new rules. The train operators should have taken the weight limits recommended by engineers seriously. The passengers didn't realize what could happen when they overloaded the train going through the tunnel. All of these mistakes led to a tragedy that could have been prevented.

Thankfully, passenger trains no longer run on coal. Technology has made communicating between train cars much easier. The lesson of these stories is that tunnels should not be treated as if they are unbreakable. The rules for tunnels are important. Tragedies don't often occur in tunnels, but when they do, they are often horrifying. We should treat these structures with the respect that they deserve and make sure to never take them for granted.

CHRONOLOGY

700 BCE The deepest and oldest qanats in the world are constructed in Gonabad, Persia.

518 BCE The first known sewage system is created in Persepolis, Iran.

25 BCE Ancient Roman engineers invent concrete.

76 CE Ancient Romans finish construction on the Via Flaminia tunnel.

1825 Sir Marc Isambard Brunel invents the first successful tunneling shield for excavating the Thames Tunnel.

1846 Henri-Joseph Maus creates the first boring machine.

1907 Carl Akeley invents shotcrete.

1945 Construction of the Delaware Aqueduct is completed.

1988 The Seikan Tunnel opens in Japan.

1994 The Channel Tunnel opens, connecting England and France underwater.

2016 The Gotthard Base Tunnel opens in Switzerland.

2017 Hyperloop One submits the most recent proposal for constructing the first submerged floating tunnel.

GLOSSARY

aqueduct A sloped tunnel designed to bring drinking water to towns and cities.

aquifer An underground layer of rock, sand, or soil that contains water.

boring method A method of constructing tunnels by using a boring machine to cut straight through the earth.

civil engineer An engineer who designs and maintains roads, bridges, tunnels, and other public works.

cut-and-cover method A method of constructing tunnels by cutting a long, deep ditch and then covering it with a roof.

immersed-tube method A method of constructing tunnels by building a fully enclosed tunnel off site and immersing it in its final location.

irrigation Using infrastructure to water crops periodically.

qanat Gently sloping underground tunnel that uses a series of wells to move water up to the surface for drinking and irrigation.

resources Important materials like coal, water, and oil that people use to improve their lives.

shotcrete Concrete sprayed from a hose onto a surface at a high velocity.

trench A long, narrow ditch.

tunnel Any man-made underground passage longer than 75 feet (23 m) and wider than 5.9 feet (1.8 m).

tunnel-boring machine A massive machine that bores circular tunnels through the earth using a cutter head and a powerful thrust system.

tunneling shield A large cylindrical structure that supports tunnel walls as they are being built.

FURTHER READING

Books

Enz, Tammy. *Structural Engineering: Learn It, Try It!* North Mankato, MN: Capstone Press, 2017.

Loh-Hagan, Virginia. *Tunnels*. Ann Arbor, MI: Cherry Lake, 2017.

Mattern, Joanne. *Tunnels.* Vero Beach, FL: Rourke Educational Media, 2015.

Moore, Jeanette. *Tunnels! With 25 Science Projects for Kids*. White River Junction, VT: Nomad Press, 2018.

Websites

Easy Science for Kids

easyscienceforkids.com/all-about-tunnels

An accessible look at the basics of tunnels, with pictures and videos.

How Stuff Works

science.howstuffworks.com/engineering/structural/tunnel.htm

A fun breakdown of the science behind tunnels.

INDEX

A

Akeley, Carl, 20

aqueducts, 8–9, 10, 32, 35, 37

aquifers, 8, 13–14

Armi tunnel, 42

B

Balvano train disaster, 41–44

boring method, 16–17, 18, 20, 29

Branson, Richard, 21

Brunel, Marc Isambard, 20

C

carbon monoxide poising, 42, 43

cave-ins, 6, 20, 24, 27

Channel Tunnel (Chunnel), 31–32, 35

Chicago flood of 1992, 39–41

cut-and-cover method, 16, 17

D

Delaware Aqueduct, 32, 35, 37

G

Gotthard Base Tunnel, 33, 35, 37

I

immersed tube method, 16, 18

K

Kinzie Street Bridge, 39

M

Martina boring machine, 18

muqannīs, 10, 22, 24

Q

qanats, 10, 22, 24

S

Seikan Tunnel, 35–37

sewer systems, 9–10

submerged floating tunnels, 20–21

T

tunnels

   disasters, 4, 6, 20, 24, 27, 38–44

   history and basic uses, 8–14

   overview, 4–7

   technology for building, 15–21

   world's coolest, 31–37

   workers, 13, 22–30

Y

Yunnan-Guizhou Water Tunnel, 37